29 Sugar Free Ic Frosting and Topping Recipes

Annie Busco The Sugar Free Diva

1st Edition

Dedication

This book is dedicated to everyone who can relate to the struggle and certainly the friends and loved ones who support the struggle. The struggle is real and the struggle is ours to beat.

Additionally, I would like to thank my fabulous family and of course, my loving fur babies.

Lastly, I wish to thank my dedicated readers. I love when my readers check in with me. They are helpful when they let me know how my recipes have worked for them and the tweaks they have made to make my recipes even better.

Forward

I have been experimenting in my kitchen with alternatives to sugar for most of my life. As expected, some experiments turned out better than others.

What you need to know about baking with sugar alternatives is that not all sugar alternatives are the same. And, while they may add the sweetness that is lost when we take sugar out of a recipe, alternatives are not chemically the same a sugar. Thus, they behave differently than sugar when used in recipes.

In most of my recipes, I suggest the kind of sugar alternative that would work best in that recipe. For example, using a granular sugar alternative that is measured the same as you would measure sugar (1:1), should not disrupt the volume of dry ingredients in a recipe like other sugar alternatives could.

There are a lot of alternatives to sugar that you can choose from to use in place of sugar in a recipe. Some sugar alternatives have their own kind of sugar yet, are used instead of common table sugar. Examples of these alternatives would include honey and molasses. They are not always the best choices for some recipes as they are sweeter than sugar and they are wet rather than dry.

Popular sugar alternatives these days include the natural sugar alternatives. An example would be sugar alternatives that are made with the Stevia. Because Stevia is so much sweeter than sugar is, less of it is needed in a recipe than sugar would be needed to achieve the same sweetness. As a result, and to keep the dry volume the same, many Stevia sweeteners are mixed with other ingredients to 'bulk' it up. Often, Stevia will be mixed with sugar.

The most common sugar alternative used by those of use who use sugar alternatives in recipes is probably a Sucralose product. Sucralose is a lot like sugar when it is baked (with a few adjustments here and there) and it is usually less expensive than most of the other alternatives.

Obviously, there are many other alternatives that you can choose from to use. If you want to learn more about baking with sugar alternatives, I have a guide "The Sugar Free Baking Guide: A must have guide for the sugar free baker " that you can find on Amazon.

You will notice in my recipes that I do not mention a certain name or brand of sugar alternative to use. I simply may suggest which kind to use for the success of a recipe. You can use the sugar alternative of your choice.

To choose the sugar alternative that would work best for you in your recipe, I suggest using one that is best for the success of the recipe. I also suggest to choose an alternative that is best for you and your body as some alternatives may not be for you. Many alternatives should be eaten in moderation, as suggested by the manufacturers and experts.

My biggest piece of advice that I could give you is to read the label on the sugar alternative packaging. Look for the ingredient label to see if there has been anything added to 'bulk up' the package. Also, look for how much of the product equals one cup of sugar in a recipe (is it 1:1 with sugar?). Lastly, look to see if that alternative will work for your kind of a recipe (especially if baking with it) and any warnings associated with the product.

Introduction

This is a book about Sugar Free Frostings, Icings and Toppings. I wrote this book because I have a lot of these kinds of recipes to share.

Let me start by telling you why I bake with sugar alternatives. I would have to first admit that I am a recovered sugar addict. While this may seem kind of funny or cute, it is real. I was (am) addicted to sugar.

My addiction started as a kid when it seems as if everything had sugar in it. There really were not a lot of sugar alternatives available at the time. Every meal and snack had sugar in it.

There was a time when sugar controlled me. Then I had to learn how to control sugar. I gave sugar up. Today, the sugar that I consume comes only from fresh fruit. I have learned how to use alternatives everywhere else.

The struggle with sugar is real. I know that the sugar struggle is there for other people besides me. Check out this research to see what I mean.

•Before there were grocery stores with prepared food (over 100 years ago basically), American's consumed about 2 pounds of sugar in a year. 2 pounds is about 192 teaspoons which would mean that Americans consumed about half a teaspoon of sugar in a day. Wow!

•50 years ago (about the time of the onset of suburbia and grocery stores) that amount of consumed sugar jumped up to over

120 pounds of sugar in a year. 11,520 teaspoons or 31 1/2 teaspoons of sugar per day.

•Today American's have decreased their consumption of sugar to as much as 20+ teaspoons of sugar daily (according to the AHA). Education and smart consumer choices have made an impact on sugar consumption according to the experts. Hence, the prior discussion about consumer demands for more of the healthy water beverages.

Clearly, I am not the only person giving up sugar.
I gave up sugar because I did not like what I call the 'Sugar Rollercoaster". The roller coaster of the sugar high that is followed to the sugar low. One minute I have a lot of energy and a short while later I need a nap.

It is not just the sugar roller coaster that turned me into a sugar free person. Sugar consumption took its toll on my weight as well as my teeth. In the end, I always felt controlled by sugar rather than me controlling the sugar.

Yes, there are a lot of sugar alternatives that you can theoretically use in a recipe. We add sugar alternatives for the purpose of achieving a sweetness like that of sugar in a recipe but, without the effect of sugar and in many cases, the calories. However, you should know that not all sugar alternatives are meant to be baked or cooked with due to their chemical makeup.

If you would like to learn more about sugar alternatives and how to use them, you can check out my book The Sugar Free Baking Guide on Amazon. I go into more depth about the many alternatives out there including the natural ones.

I prefer a granular sugar alternative in most of my recipes. You will see 'granular' in the ingredient listing to let you know that you should be using it as well. A granular sugar alternative is more like sugar when it comes to the dry ingredient volume in a recipe. There are plenty of granular choices for you to choose from which include the natural and artificial ones.

You will also notice that I will list a sugar alternative ingredient as 1:1 with sugar. That means if you would normally use 1 cup of sugar in the recipe, your alternative would also measure out as 1 cup. The best way to know for sure that your alternative is 1:1 to sugar is to read the label on the package. Also note if your product has been filled to get it to a 1:1 equivalence as sugar is sometimes used with the sugar alternative.

I will rarely suggest a specific product to use. I may however say that a certain product wold work best in a specific recipe. People can be, understandably, partial to a specific product or whether or not it is a natural product.

Many sugar alternatives can have an effect you. If you are sensitive to a sugar alternative you should avoid it or consume it in moderation. I only had to learn that lesson once.

Let me take a moment to discuss some of the dairy ingredients used in recipes in this book.

I love using Greek Yogurt in recipes. Preferable, the low fat stuff that has no added flavor or sugar in it. Greek Yogurt can be used as a thicker dairy ingredient, sometimes alone or sometimes when mixed with other ingredients. I mention in my recipes when Greek Yogurt can be used.

Greek Yogurt could be used as an alternative to heavy whipping cream by adding a bit of cornstarch (2 tsp) or flour (1 tbsp) to 1 cup of it. Or mix the yogurt 1:1 with whole milk.

I like to offer ideas for alternatives in just about ever recipe that I write. For many dairy products, there are vegan alternatives that are available. For example you could use almond milk or vegan cream cheese in many of these recipes. I am not vegan and thus, I am not an expert on this.

When it comes to using sugar alternatives in place of sugar in any recipes, pretty much all recipes, there is going to be trial and error. Sugar alternatives really only replace the sweetness in a recipe that would have come from sugar.

Sugar alternatives are not chemically the same as sugar. Sometimes, especially when you are baking or cooking, you may need to make adjustments in your recipes. These adjustments include in wet ingredients or baking/cooking times or temperatures.

Another factor that can affect how your recipe turns out can include your weather. If it is dry where you are then your recipe can come out a bit dry. On the flip side, if it is moist in your location then your recipe may hold on to moisture better.

I start this book with recipes for Sugar Free Powdered Sugar and

Sugar Free Whipped Cream. These recipes are seen throughout this book as ingredients in other recipes. Putting these recipes first will help you refer to them when you need to make them in order to make them in other recipes.

Use your imagination on some of these recipes to tweak your results. You do not always need to make your extract vanilla for example. Or you could add a drop or two of food coloring to make them pretty.

As mentioned, I start this book with recipes for Sugar Free Powdered Sugar and Sugar Free Whipped Cream. This is because these results of these recipes are used as ingredients in other recipes throughout this book.

The remaining recipes are grouped according to likeness. I start with frostings. Nearly half of this book is devoted to frosting recipes. There are so many ways to make a good frosting for every kind of baked goodies.

Then we will move on to icings and glazes. While icings and glazes are not necessarily frostings, they are alternatives just the same. We can top a great cake or cupcake with a frosting, icing or glaze.

The remainder of this book is devoted to other recipes for topping ideas. I also have fillings, dips, and recipes that can be used as ingredients in other recipes. The final recipes, Sugar Free Marshmallows, is one of my most popular recipes on thesugarfreediva.com.

How to Make Sugar Free Powdered Sugar

I am starting sugar free powdered sugar because we will see this pop up as an ingredient in other recipes throughout this cookbook. Making your own powdered sugar is actually easier to do than you may have expected. However, if you are wanting to buy this already made, it is available online as well.

Sugar Free Powdered Sugar

Here is what you need to make Sugar Free Powdered Sugar.

Method 1.

- Granular Sugar Alternative (I use a Sucralose brand)- 3/4 cup
- Cornstarch- 2 tablespoons.

Simply sift together your ingredients into a bowl.

Method 2.

- Sugar Free Nonfat Dry Milk Powder- 2 cups
- Cornstarch- 2 cups
- Granular Sugar Alternative- 1 cup

Use a blender or food processor to blend these ingredients together until well blended.

Method 3.

- Using a Baking Blend of a Granular Sugar Alternative- 1 cup
- Cornstarch- 1 teaspoon.

Blend or process on high until blended.

Sugar Free Whipped Cream

Whipped cream is another ingredient that I use often in recipes. Since it is pretty close to impossible to find any with low or no sugar in it, I decided to make my own.

What you will need to make Sugar Free Whipped Cream.

- Heavy Whipped Cream- 1 cup.
- Granular Sugar Alternative or Sugar Free Powdered Sugar- 3 tablespoons.
- Vanilla Extract- 1 teaspoon

How to make Sugar Free Whipped Cream.

1. Use a metal mixing bowl and a whisk to make this. Start by placing the metal bowl and the whisk in your freezer for 20 minutes.

2. Remove the mixing bowl and whisk from the freezer and place your ingredients in the bowl.

3. Whisk the ingredients together until peaks begin to form. Do not over whisk.

Make this recipe even more interesting by using an extract other than vanilla.

Sugar Free Buttercream Frosting

This is really one of my most popular recipes. I think the popularity of this recipe has to do with the usability of this. That is, a basic buttercream frosting that can go with just about any kind of a cake. Plus, it is pretty tasty. I will offer other versions of buttercream

Sugar Free Buttercream Frosting

frostings in this book. Here is the basic go-to buttercream frosting recipe.

What you will need to make Sugar Free Butter Cream Frosting.

- Sugar Free Powdered Sugar- 3 cups.
- Butter (salted or unsalted)- 1 cup (2 sticks) softened to room temperature.
- Milk or similar dairy- 1-2 teaspoons.

How to make Sugar Free Butter Cream Frosting.

1.   In a mixing bowl, cream together the sugar free powdered sugar and the butter. I use a paddle attachment for this.

2.   Start mixing on low and then after a minute until somewhat blended and the increase the speed to medium for 2 1/2- 3 minutes until blended.

3.   Scrape the sides of the bowl and then add the remaining ingredients.

4.   Continue mixing on medium for 1- 1 1/2 minutes until you reach a good texture and all is blended.

The dairy that you choose to use in this recipe will affect the final consistency and taste. For example, using skim milk will save you a few calories but, with yield a thinner texture and lighter taste. Buttermilk will offer a thicker and richer taste with a few more calories. I tend to stick to something in the middle for this recipe.

Stevia Cream Cheese Frosting

I seem to get a lot of requests for recipes that use Stevia sweeteners. Since Stevia is sweeter than other sweeteners, less of it is needed in most recipes. Granular Pure Stevia is recommended in this recipe. This is a great recipe to use with carrot cake.

Stevia Cream Cheese Frosting

What you will need to make Stevia Cream Cheese Frosting.

- Cream Cheese- 1 8 ounce package softened to room temperature.
- Butter- 1/4 cup softened to room temperature.
- Milk or similar dairy- 1-2 tablespoons depending on desired consistency.
- Stevia - 1 teaspoon and increase as needed. Pure Stevia granular is recommended.
- Vanilla Extract- 1 teaspoon.

How to make Stevia Cream Cheese Frosting.

1. In a mixing bowl cream together the cream cheese and butter. I use a paddle attachment on low-medium for this.

2. When creamed, switch to a whisk or whisk attachment. Add a tablespoon of milk and a tablespoon of Stevia as well as the vanilla extract. Whisk on medium for a minute stop and test for taste and consistency.

3. Add additional milk and Stevia as needed until you reach your desired sweetness and consistency.

This is generally a rich in consistency frosting. Adding the additional tablespoon of milk will make this easier to pipe.

Chocolate Cream Cheese Frosting

This is the chocolate version of the cream cheese frosting that we just touched on. This frosting is rich and is perfect for birthday cakes and delicious cupcakes. We will be using unsweetened cocoa and sugar free powdered sugar in this recipe. Please note that there is also a Cocoa Buttercream Frosting recipe in this book that is just a

Sugar Free Chocolate Cream Cheese Frosting

bit different from this one as it contains no cream cheese and may be easier to convert to a vegan recipe.

What you will need to make Chocolate Cream Cheese Frosting.

- Unsweetened Powdered Cocoa- 1/2 cup.
- Sugar Free Powdered Sugar- 3 cups.
- Butter- 1 stick (1/2 cup) softened.
- Cream Cheese- 1 8 ounce package softened.
- Vanilla Extract- 1 teaspoon.
- Milk or similar dairy- 1 -2 tablespoons as needed.

How to make Chocolate Cream Cheese Frosting.

1. In a small bowl, whisk or sift together the unsweetened cocoa powder and the sugar free powdered sugar. Set this aside.

2. Next, in a mixing bowl blend together the butter and cream cheese. I use a paddle attachment on low-medium for about a minute to a minute and a half.

3.   Add the cocoa and powdered sugar to the mixing bowl along with the vanilla extract and a tablespoon of milk to the mixing bowl. Mix on low until smooth without lumps. I suggest stopping at some point(s) as needed to scrape the sides of the bowl.

4.   Add an additional tablespoon as needed to thin this out if needed.

I was just thinking how this frosting would taste amazing as a dip too. I have a recipe for sugar free graham crackers on my site that would be perfect in this.

Sugar Free Cocoa Buttercream Frosting

This is a similar recipe to the Chocolate Cream Cheese Frosting recipe in this book. This recipe features butter which can easily be converted to vegan as well. I like this recipe for the occasions that I would rather have a frosting that is not as rich as a cream cheese frosting.

Sugar Free Cocoa Buttercream Frosting

What you need for this Sugar Free Cocoa Buttercream Frosting.

- Butter- 6 tablespoons, creamed/softened.
- Sugar Free Powdered Sugar- 2 2/3 cups.
- Unsweetened Cocoa Powder- 1/3 cup.
- Vanilla Extract- 2 teaspoons.
- Milk or Cream- 1 1/2 teaspoon.

How to make Sugar Free Cocoa Buttercream Frosting

1. Cream the butter if it is not already creamed. I use room softened butter and place in a mixer on low-medium for about a minute. If the butter is already very soft, creaming it by hand should be easy to do with a fork.

2. In a small bowl, combine together the sugar free powdered sugar and the unsweetened cocoa powder. You can use a whisk or sifter to do this.

3. Blend together the butter and the powdered sugar/cocoa mixture. Then add the vanilla extract and the milk. I use a mixing bowl and a paddle attachment on low-medium. You could probably do this effectively by hand as well. Be sure to scrape the sides of the bowl as needed.

Sugar Free Greek Yogurt Frosting

Unsweetened low fat Greek Yogurt has certainly been my friend. I can eat it alone, with fruit, frozen, or as part of a recipe such as this one. In this recipe, the yogurt will be used with cream cheese to make a great frosting. If you are wanting to make a good frosting that is a healthier choice, you could use a cream cheese alternative. This frosting may not be as rich as a regular frosting but, it will be a good choice for many.

Sugar Free Frosting Made With Greek Yogurt

What you will need to make Sugar Free Greek Yogurt

- Greek Yogurt- 1 cup. I use the unsweetened low fat Greek Yogurt. To strain, place a strainer over a cup or glass. Line the strainer with a coffee filter, strong paper towel or cheese cloth. Place the yogurt over the lined strainer and allow this to sit overnight in the refrigerator.
- Sugar Free Powdered Sugar- 1 1/4 cups.
- Cream Cheese- 1 8 ounce package softened
- Vanilla Extract- 1 teaspoon.

How to make Sugar Free Greek Yogurt

1. Use as strained yogurt as described above. Strain if not already strained.

2. Whip together the yogurt and the powdered sugar.

3. Add the cream cheese and vanilla extract and cream the ingredients until the ingredients are blended and you have a good consistency.

While I use Greek Yogurt and vanilla extract, I am wondering how a flavored yogurt would work in this recipe. Simply omit the vanilla extract if you decide to try this idea.

Sugar Free Cocoa Frosting made with Greek Yogurt

This is really a great frosting when you are looking for something chocolate and not really heavy. I like the way that the Greek Yogurt works with the cocoa in this recipe. Straining the yogurt in this recipe is optional. If you want a thicker consistency, you could certainly strain the yogurt first .

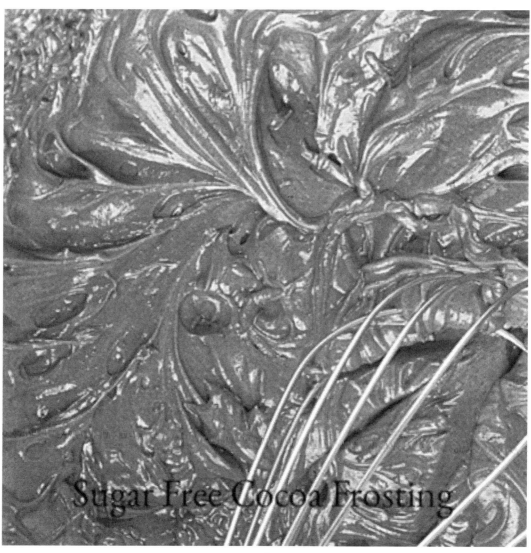

Sugar Free Cocoa Frosting

What you will need to make Sugar Free Cocoa Frosting made with Greek Yogurt.

- Unsweetened Cocoa Powder- 1/2 cup.
- Sugar Free Powdered Sugar- 2 cups.
- Butter- 1/2 cup (1 stick).
- Sugar Free Chocolate Chips- 1/2 cup.
- Vanilla Extract- 1 teaspoon.
- Cream Cheese- 1 tablespoon.
- Greek Yogurt- 1/3 cup, strained as desired.

How to make Sugar Free Cocoa Frosting made with Greek Yogurt.

1.   Sift or whisk together the unsweetened cocoa powder and sugar free powdered sugar in a medium bowl. Set this aside.

2.   Melt together the butter and sugar free chocolate chips, If using a microwave, use a microwave-safe bowl or cup. Microwave for a minute to a minute and a half, stirring every 30 seconds, until melted. On the stove, melt on low stirring continuously.

3.   Allow the melted chocolate and butter to cool for a minute and then transfer it to a mixing bowl. Add

the unsweetened cocoa powder and powdered sugar to the bowl and gently mix.

4.   Add the vanilla extract and cream cheese to the mixing bowl and mix for about a minute.

5.   Finally, stir in the Greek Yogurt. Whip or mix this frosting until you reach your desired consistency..

Sugar free chocolate chips can easily be found online. I use them in a number of my recipes.

Sugar Free and Pudding Cream Cheese Frosting

Adding pudding is really a great hack for a recipe such as this one. After all, pudding comes in a variety of flavors. By the way, when you use pudding, make sure that it is sugar free and powdered (not already made).

Sugar Free Pudding and Cream Cheese Frosting

Since the weight of sugar free instant pudding packages differs from the regular stuff, look for a four serving size. Also, an optional ingredient in this recipe is whipped topping. Earlier in this book, there was a recipe for sugar free whipped topping that you could use in this recipe.

What is needed in this Sugar Free and Pudding Cream Cheese Frosting recipe.

Sugar Free Instant Pudding- 1 four serving box. Any flavor.

Milk or similar dairy- 1 cup.

Cream Cheese- 1 8 ounce package softened.

Vanilla Extract- 1 teaspoon. This can be omitted depending on the flavor of pudding used.

Optional- Sugar Free Whipped Topping.- 1 cup.

How to make Sugar Free Pudding and Cream Cheese Frosting

1. Whisk together the sugar free instant pudding and the milk.

2. Add the cream cheese and vanilla extract and whip or beat until you reach your desired consistency.

3. If you are using the whipped topping you can sub it in for the milk or add it in addition to the milk or use 1/2 cup of each. The whipped topping is good for

a colder recipe such as a frozen cheesecake. Using both whipped topping and milk will yield a thinner frosting.

I actually do use this recipe for a frozen low carb sugar free cheesecake. I do not use milk in my recipe when I use whipped topping.

Sugar Free Gelatin Frosting

A box of gelatin used as an ingredient is the perfect hack in this recipe. Not only does the gelatin bring us some flavor and a bit of ingredient binding, it also provides us with color. By gelatin, I mean that box of instant gelatin that we all know of. Choose the flavor of your choice and a sugar free gelatin box that has four servings.

Sugar Free Frosting Made With Gelatin

What is needed to make Sugar Free Gelatin Frosting

- Cream Cheese- 1 8 ounce package, softened to room temperature.

- Butter- 1 stick (1/2 cup) also soft.

- Sugar Free Gelatin- 1 box (4 servings). Any flavor and/or color.

- Sugar Free Powdered Sugar- 3 cups.

- Whipping Cream or tubbed whip cream or even Greek Yogurt- 2 1/2 tablespoons.

How to make Sugar Free Gelatin Frosting

1. Start by blending together the cream cheese and butter in a mixing bowl.

2. When blended, stir in the gelatin.

3. Next, add the powdered sugar. I use a paddle attachment and my mixer set on medium to medium low to blend this in.

4. Then, whisk in the dairy (whipping cream, tubbed whip cream, or Greek Yogurt). Whip until fluffy.

5. Refrigerate this frosting. If you are making this frosting in advance and to serve later, simply

refrigerate after the third step and add the dairy just before serving.

If you are looking for an easy way to cut out some of the fat and calories, try a lower fat version of the cream cheese. The texture of the frosting may not be as rich however.

Sugar Free Strawberry Buttercream Frosting 1.

I actually have two methods of making this. There is the fresh strawberry version and then the instant pudding version. Both are worth a try when you are looking for a strawberry buttercream frosting. This first method is with fresh strawberries. Strawberries are fairly low in sugar in case you were wondering.

Sugar Free Strawberry Buttercream Frosting 1

What you will need to make Sugar Free Strawberry Buttercream frosting.

- Strawberries- 1/2 cup, about 4-5 strawberries whole and with stems removed.
- Cream Cheese- 1 8 ounce package soft.
- Butter- 1 stick (1/2 cup) cut into tablespoons.
- Sugar Free Powdered Sugar- 3 1/2 cups.
- Vanilla Extract- 1 teaspoon.

How to make Sugar Free Strawberry Frosting Method 1

1. Use a blender or food processor to puree the strawberries.

2. In a mixing bowl, blend together the cream cheese and butter.

3. When creamy, add the sugar free powdered sugar and vanilla extract. Mix this on low.

4. When blended, mix in the strawberries. Whip until you reach your desired consistency.

Sugar Free Buttercream Strawberry Frosting 2

This is the cheat method for making strawberry frosting. I am going to make this fun by adding some Greek Yogurt (I use the fat free no sugar added stuff).

Sugar Free Buttercream Frosting 2

What you will need to make Sugar Free Strawberry Frosting 2

- Cream Cheese- 1 8 ounce package softened . Can sub in 4 ounces of butter for 4 ounces of cream cheese if you want that butter taste and consistency.

- Greek Yogurt, Milk, or heavy Whipping Cream - 1 cup. What you use depends on the consistency, fat, and calories you want.

- Sugar Free Strawberry Instant Pudding- 1 box (4 servings).

- Vanilla Extract- 1 teaspoon (can omit if you do not want a vanilla taste).

How to make Sugar Free Strawberry Frosting with Pudding

1.   Blend together the cream cheese and Greek Yogurt in a mixer.

2.   Add the remaining ingredients and whip or blend until you reach your desired consistency.

3.   If your frosting seems to be too thing, simply add a bit more of the cream cheese or butter to thicken it.

Sugar Free White Chocolate Frosting

This is another one of my pudding frosting recipe ideas. When I saw that there is a sugar free white chocolate instant pudding, I was all over this one. This frosting goes with about any kind of cake-including chocolate or carrot.

Sugar Free White Chocolate Frosting

What you will need to make Sugar Free White Chocolate Frosting

- Sugar Free White Chocolate Instant Pudding- 2 boxes (8 servings)
- Sugar Free Powdered Sugar- 2 1/2 cups
- Butter- 2 sticks (1 cup) soft.
- Vanilla Extract- 1 teaspoon.
- Whipping Cream- 1 1/2 tablespoon.

How to make Sugar Free White Chocolate Frosting

1. I use a whisk attachment. Cream together the pudding, powdered sugar, and butter on low.

2. When blended (about a minute) increase the speed to medium and whisk until fluffy. This could take a few minutes to achieve desired 'fluffiness'.

3. Add the remaining ingredients (vanilla extract and whipping cream) and whip for another minute to minute and a half.

4. If needed, you can adding additional cream.

This makes a bit more frosting than most of the other recipes in this book. You could easily freeze leftovers or refrigerate them for later us.

4 Ingredient Sugar Free Vanilla Frosting

What could be more simple that a recipe that has only four ingredients in it? This is that 'quicky' frosting recipe that you can whip up in a pinch. Or, if you really like it, use it for about anything.

4 Ingredient Sugar Free Frosting

What you need to make Sugar Free 4 Ingredient Sugar Free Vanilla Frosting

- Sugar Free Powdered Sugar- 2 1/2- 3 cups. Start with 2 1/2 and add additional powdered sugar as needed.
- Milk- 2 tablespoons
- Butter- 2 sticks (1 cup) soft.
- Vanilla Extract- 1 teaspoon

How to make 4 Ingredient Sugar Free Vanilla Frosting

1. If your butter is really soft, you can simply add all of the ingredients to your mix and whip this up until fluffy. I start on low for about a minute and then increase the speed a bit (medium).

2. However, if your butter is not really soft, simply cream it in the mixer and then add the other ingredients to whip up until fluffy.

3. If your frosting seems to be a bit thin, add additional powdered sugar a bit at a time until you reach a good consistency.

Really, this is meant to be a quick an easy frosting to make. As long as your butter is soft, you can pretty much put everything in the mixer and mix until fluffy (a few minutes). Why not switch in another flavor extract for the vanilla for an added taste?

5 Ingredient Sugar Free Cream Cheese Frosting

This is a quick and easy recipe just like the last one was. The difference between the two (besides this recipe having an extra ingredient) is that this recipe is not made with powdered sugar. Instead, the ingredients for powdered sugar are part of the recipe itself.

5 Ingredient Cream Cheese Frosting

What you need to make 5 Ingredient Sugar Free Cream Cheese Frosting

- Sugar Alternative- 4 cups, granulated.
- Cornstarch- 6 tablespoons.
- Butter- 1 stick (1/2 cup) softened
- Cream Cheese- 1 8 ounce package, soft.
- Vanilla Extract- 2 teaspoons

How to make 5 Ingredient Sugar Free Cream Cheese Frosting

1. Start by sifting together the sugar alternative and cornstarch. Set this aside .

2. In a mixer, cream together the butter and cream cheese.

3. Add the sugar alternative and cornstarch mix to the mixing bowl and then the vanilla extract. Whip or blend until you get your desired consistency.

This recipe would also be great with another kind of extract too. Or, why not try some food coloring?

Royal Icing with Stevia

This is the perfect recipe for icing that can be used to decorate your holiday cookies or breakfast cake. Stevia is popular with many of my readers.

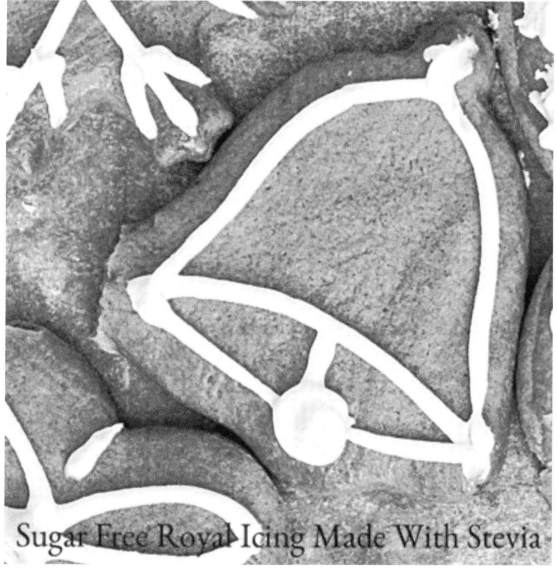

Sugar Free Royal Icing Made With Stevia

What you need for Royal Icing with Stevia

- Stevia Baking Blend- 3 cups
- Cornstarch- 3 teaspoons
- Meringue Powder- 3 teaspoons
- Vanilla Extract- 1 teaspoons
- Water- 1/2 cup

How to make Royal Icing with Stevia

1. Start by sifting together the Stevia Baking Blend and the cornstarch. Set this aside.

2. Now, in a mixing bowl, whisk together the water, vanilla, and meringue powder. Whisk this until you see peaks form.

3. I use a paddle attachment for this next step. Add the ingredients from the first bowl (sifted Stevia and cornstarch) to the mixing bowl.

4. Mix until blended.

5. This should result in something that is easy to pipe or decorate with. If you need to thin this out, simply add a teaspoon or so of water.

Divide the mix and add food coloring to make this even prettier!

Sugar Free Royal Icing with Splenda

Here is another Royal Icing recipe only this one uses Splenda as a sweetener. Use this Royal Icing for your holiday cookies or for sliced fruit for fun!

What you need to make Sugar Free Royal Icing with Splenda

- Meringue Powder OR Pasteurized Egg Whites- 6 teaspoons.
- Vanilla Extract- 1 teaspoon.
- Splenda Granular- 4 cups
- Cornstarch- 1/2 cup
- Warm Water- 1/3 cup (omit if using egg whites)

How to make Sugar Free Royal Icing with Splenda

1. Combine the egg whites (if using meringue powder, see below) and the vanilla extract in a mixing bowl. Beat until this gets frothy.

2. Add the Splenda and the cornstarch to the mixing bowl and mix on low for 30 seconds.

3. After 30 seconds you can turn the speed up to to medium and mix until peaks form. This could take 5-7 minutes for the peaks to form.

4. EGG WHITE METHOD- Beat the pasteurized egg whites, vanilla extract, Splenda Granular, and cornstarch on low until blended.

5.   Then add the water and beat on low until peaks form.

Both methods can be easily thinned out with a bit of water. Be sure to refrigerate this icing as well.

Sugar Free Glaze

You've just made your sugar free donut and now you need something to top it off with. That is just one reason why there us a Sugar Free Glaze. This is one of those great ways that we can imitate sugar using sugar alternative.

What you need to make Sugar Free Glaze

- Sugar Free Granular Alternative- 3/4 cup equivalent to sugar.
- Cornstarch- 2 tablespoons.
- Water or milk- 2 teaspoons.
- Vanilla Extract- 1/2 teaspoon.

How to make Sugar Free Glaze

1. Start by sifting together the sugar free granular alternative and the cornstarch.

2. Add the liquid (water or milk) a teaspoon at a time, stirring between additions.

3. Then stir in the vanilla extract.

4. If this seems a bit thin for your needs, add a bit of granular alternative that has been sifted with cornstarch. Add a teaspoon at a time.

Make this even more fun by adding a drop or two of food coloring.

Sugar Free Chocolate Glaze

It was when I posted my recipe for a Sugar Free Boston Cream Pie Cake that I realized that there was a need for a Sugar Free Chocolate Glaze. You will need a corn syrup alternative for this. If you go to thesugarfreediva.com you can find alternative ideas (do a search for Sugar Free Chocolate Glaze)

What you need to make Sugar Free Chocolate Glaze

- Sugar Free Chocolate Chips- 1 cup.
- Butter- 1/4 cup (half stick).
- Corn Syrup Alternative- 1/4 cup.
- Vanilla Extract- 1/2 teaspoon.

How to make Sugar Free Chocolate Glaze.

1. Microwave Method- Use a microwave safe cup or bowl. Place the chocolate chips and butter in the cup or bowl and microwave for one minute- stopping to stir half way through (30 seconds). Add the remaining ingredients (Corn Syrup Alternative and Vanilla Extract) and microwave till blended and melted- stirring every 30 seconds. This should take no longer than 3 minutes total to reach your desired consistency.

2. Double Boiler Method- Fill the bottom of the boiler with 2 1/2- 3 inches of water and bring to a boil. Turn the heat down to medium and place the top of the boiler. Melt the chocolate chips and butter, stirring consistently. Then stir in the remaining ingredient, stirring and not allowing to bubble or stick.

For fun, add a bit of rum or alternative extract instead of the vanilla extract. Sugar Free Cream Filling

Sugar Free Cream Filling

It was when I was making one of those sugar free sandwich cookies that I realized there was a need for this. I like that this is an easy recipe that is also a lot like its sugar cousin.

Sugar Free Cream Filling

What you need to make Sugar Free Cream Filling

- Butter- 2 sticks (1 cup) softened.
- Sugar Free Powdered Sugar- 2 cups.
- Vanilla Extract- 2 teaspoons.
- Optional- sub in 1 8 ounce softened cream cheese for a stick of butter for an even more creamy result.
- Optional- heavy cream or milk, a teaspoon at a time, can thin this out if needed.

How to make Sugar Free Cream Filling

1. Cream together the butter and sugar free powdered sugar.

2. Add the vanilla extract and whip until fluffy and creamy.

3. Add optional dairy a teaspoon at a time to thin this if needed.

Add 2 teaspoons of unsweetened cocoa plus a teaspoon or two of dairy to make this a cocoa filling.

Sugar Free Chocolate Hard Shell Topping

For those of us who are fans of ice cream, there is a way to put a hard shell on it. All sugar free of course. There are only three ingredients in this too!

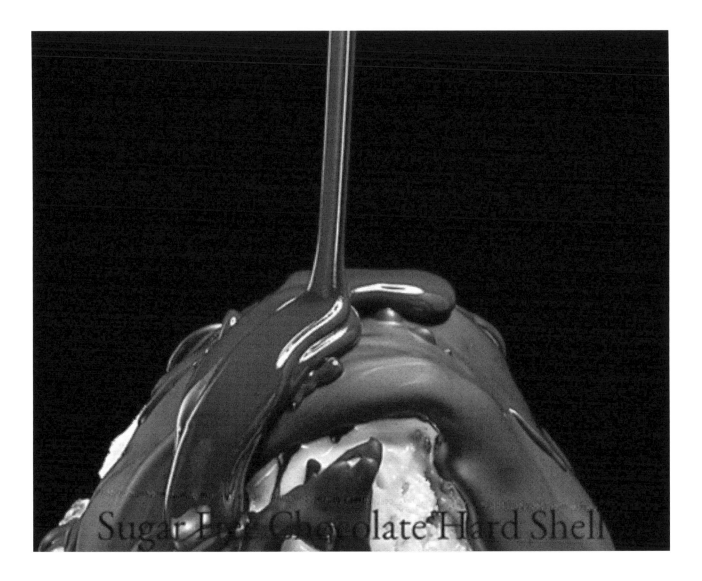

What you need to make Sugar Free Chocolate Hard Shell Topping

- Sugar Free Chocolate Chips- 1 bag (8-10 ounces).
- Edible Coconut Oil-1/4 cup.
- Vanilla Extract- 1/2 teaspoon.

Sugar Free Chocolate Shell Topping

1. In a saucepan on medium-low heat, combine all of the ingredients.

2. Cover and stir frequently, scraping the bottom of the saucepan as needed to prevent burning and promote blending.

3. When the ingredients appear to be melted and combined (4-5 minutes), remove the saucepan from the stove.

4. Allow the mixture to cool for a moment before covering your ice cream to prevent melting the ice cream (gasp!).

5. This should harden on the ice cream in about a minute after covering the ice cream,

Add some chopped nuts to the sauce pan after removing it from the heat or sprinkle them on top before the shell hardens.

Sugar Free Chocolate Fondue

This Sugar Free Chocolate Fondue is especially popular around Valentine's Day. I am a strawberry dipper myself.

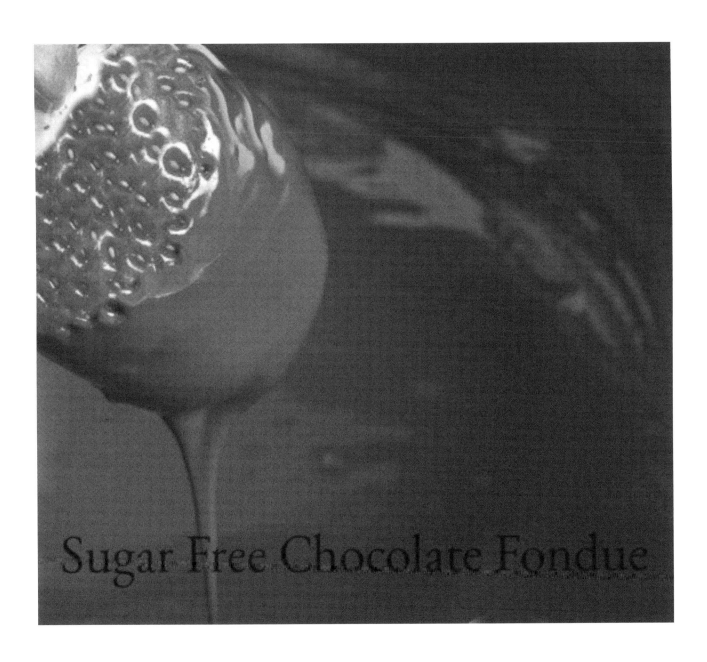

What you need to make Sugar Free Chocolate Fondue

Sugar Free Chocolate Chips- 1 cup.

Heavy Cream- 2/3 cup.

Vanilla Extract- 1 tablespoon.

How to make Sugar Free Chocolate Fondue

1.   Double boiler method- add water to the bottom boiler and allow to bubble. Turn the heat down to medium and add the heavy cream. Stir continuously. When this begins to bubble, remove from heat and stir in the chocolate chips and extract.

2.   Single sauce pan method- in a sauce pan set on medium heat, warm the chocolate chips and heavy cream, stirring consistently. Once melted, remove from heat and stir in the vanilla extract.

3.   Microwave method- obviously, use a microwave safe bowl. Combine all ingredients in your microwave safe bowl and microwave on high for a minute. Stir and continue to microwave until blended- stirring every 30 seconds of course.

Transfer this to a fondue pot and serve with strawberries, marshmallow, etc.

Sugar Free Chocolate Syrup

Chocolate syrup is that perfect topping for a sundae or some delicious waffles. This chocolate syrup has no added sugar in it. By the way, this would be a great tasting chocolate dip as well!

What you need to make Sugar Free Chocolate Syrup

- Unsweetened Cocoa Powder- 3/4 cup.
- Water, Milk, or Almond Milk- 1 1/4 cup. Your choice should have something to do with your desired consistency and of course, nutritional elements.
- Sugar Alternative- Equivalent to 1/2 cup of sugar. Since dry volume is not a factor in this recipe, you could use the alternative that works best for you. It does not have to be a granular sugar alternative.
- Vanilla Extract- 2 teaspoons.

How to make Sugar Free Chocolate Syrup

1. In a large sauce pan on medium heat whisk together the cocoa powder and milk (liquid). You will need to continuously whisk this as you want to break up any lumps.

2. When the mixture begins to boil, bump the heat down to a medium-low setting. Allow this to sit for 3-4 minutes, stirring as needed, until the mixture has thickened somewhat.

3. Remove from heat and stir in the remaining ingredients (sugar alternative and vanilla extract).

4. Store this in the refrigerator.

Sugar Free Caramel Sauce

I must admit, the first time that I enjoyed a caramel sauce was when my daughter was young and we were invited to a fall mother-daughter gathering. Our host served a most spectacular treat of sliced apples with caramel sauce dip. The apples and caramel made for the perfect pairing of fall goodness!

What you need to make Sugar Free Caramel Sauce

- Unsalted Butter- 1/2 cup (1 stick).
- Sugar Alternative- 1/3 cup + 1 tablespoon equivalent to sugar, granular.
- Brown Sugar Alternative- 2 tablespoons, equivalent to brown sugar.
- Heavy Cream- 1/2 cup.
- Salt- pinch.
- Vanilla Extract- 1 teaspoon.
- Water- 2 tablespoons + additional as needed.

How to make Sugar Free Caramel Sauce

1. Preheat a medium saucepan on medium heat.

2. When warm, about 4-5 minutes, add the butter to the saucepan.

3. When the butter has mostly melted, stir in the sugar alternatives (granular and brown). Stir this continuously to prevent burning or overcooking.

4. When the ingredients in the saucepan begin to bubble, (about 4-5 minutes) you can remove the saucepan from the heat.

5. Whisk in the heavy cream and then return the saucepan to the stove. Heat the saucepan on medium heat. When it begins to bubble again, you can remove the saucepan from the heat and stir in the vanilla extract.

6. Allow this to cool before serving.

While apples and ice cream are the perfect pair for this, saltine crackers may also work well.

Sugar Free Chocolate Whipped Cream

I am one of those silly people who could actually eat Sugar Free Chocolate Whipped Cream by itself. Sugar Free Chocolate Whipped Cream would also taste great with some fruit or on top of a basic cake.

Sugar Free Chocolate Whipped Cream

What you need to make Sugar Free Chocolate Whipped Cream

- Heavy Cream or Whipping Cream- 1/2 cup. Going easy on the fat content with your choice can affect the consistency of the whipped cream.
- Unsweetened Cocoa Powder, 1 tablespoon. You can add more as needed for a richer taste.
- Vanilla Extract- 1 teaspoon.
- Sugar Alternative- 1 1/2 teaspoon equivalent to sugar. Granular is my preference in this recipe. Sugar free powdered sugar also works well in this recipe.

How to make Sugar Free Chocolate Whipped Cream

1. There are two ways to start this recipe. The first way is to place your mixing bowl and mixer beater attachments in the refrigerator for at least 30 minutes. Remove the mixing bowl and and attachments and gently stir in the ingredients. Skip to step 3.

2. The second method is to gently stir the ingredients together in your mixing bowl. Then place the mixing bowl and the beater in the refrigerator for 30 minutes.

3.   For both methods continue here. Outfit your mixer the refrigerated beaters. Beat the ingredients on high until peaks form. This should take about 3 1/2 - 4 minutes.

Add some fun to this recipe by substituting a flavored extract or a bit of rum for the the vanilla extract.

How to Make Sugar Free Sprinkles

I had searched everywhere for Sugar Free Sprinkles. When I could not find them I decided to make my own Sugar Free Sprinkles. There are a couple of ingredients on the list that you may not have in your panty.

Sugar Free Sprinkles

What you need to make Sugar Free Sprinkles

- Sugar Free Powdered Sugar- 2 cups.
- Pasteurized Egg Whites- 2 tablespoons.
- Vanilla Extract-1 teaspoon.
- Water- as needed, up to 1 1/2 teaspoons total.
- Food Coloring- drops as needed.
- Plastic Baggies- as needed.

How to make Sugar Free Sprinkles.

1. Start by prepping a baking sheet or similar pan with parchment paper. Set this aside as you work.

2. Whisk together the the powdered sugar and the pasteurized eggs whites in a medium mixing bowl.

3. Add the vanilla extract and 1/2 teaspoon of water to the mix and stir. Then continue adding water in very small amounts until a paste forms.

4. Divide the paste up into smaller bowls, depending on the number of different colored sprinkles that you desire. Add a drop or drops of food coloring to each bowl until your reach your desired colors.

5. In this step, we will bag each of the colored pastes that we have made in order to pipe our sprinkles on to the prepped baking sheet. Place the

first bowl of colored paste into a plastic bag and seal the bag. Snip off a corner of the bag with a scissors. We will use this opened corner to make the sprinkles so if you want small sprinkles, make your snip a small one. If you want larger sprinkles, make your snip larger.

6.   In this step we will pipe the paste on to the parchment paper. You can do this in dots (for circles) or in strips that you can cut or break done later.

7.   Allow your sprinkles to dry overnight in the refrigerator. Then, remove from the refrigerator and cut the strips into pieces or whatever you may want.

8.   I store mine in the refrigerator.

I love a recipe that can be used for anything from cupcakes to ice cream. This would be that recipe.

Sugar Free Hazelnut Spread

This is the 'copycat' version of that famous hazelnut spread that people seem to enjoy eating. If you have ever read the ingredient label on that spread then you know there is a good amount of sugar in it too. This hazelnut spread is the version without all of that added sugar.

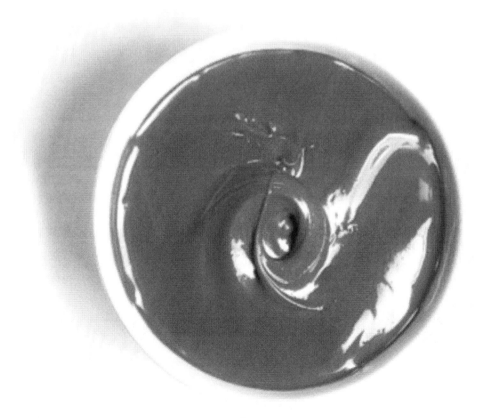

Sugar Free Hazelnut Spread

What you need to make Sugar Free Hazelnut Spread

- Roasted Hazelnuts- 1 cup and skinned. You can actually buy these online.

- Canola Oil- 1 teaspoon.

- Sugar Alternative- 1 tablespoon equivalent to sugar.

- Sugar Free Chocolate Chips- 1 cup melted OR unsweetened cocoa powder- 1/2 cup.

- Greek Yogurt- 1 tablespoon. Can sub in heavy cream or evaporated milk (there is a recipe for sugar free evaporated milk on thesugarfreediva.com).

How to make Sugar Free Hazelnut Spread

1.   In a food processor, or blender that can be used as one, process the hazlenuts and the oil until a paste forms. This should take about a minute.

2.   To the processor, add the sugar alternative and if using cocoa, the cocoa. Process this until blended. You will need to stop at some point midway while processing to scape the sides of the container.

3.   If using the chocolate chip method, add the meted chips to the processor and pulse until blended.

This hazelnut spread can be used as a spread or as an ingredient is something else such as a frosting.

Sugar Free Lemon Curd

I was a late bloomer in the lemon curd department. But, the truth is that there is a lot that can be done using lemon curd. Being a fan of lemon and of pies, I am now a fan.

What you need to make Sugar Free Lemon Curd

- No Sugar Added Lemon Juice- 1/2 cup. Squeezing your own is the best way to insure that there has been no sugar added. That would be somewhere between 2-3 lemon, depending on the size of the lemons.
- Lemon Zest- 2 1/2 teaspoons grated. You can buy this online or it would take less than one lemon to grate your own zest.
- Sugar Alternative- Equivalent to 1/2 cup of sugar. Most alternatives could work in this recipe.
- Eggs- 3.
- Butter- 6 tablespoons, cubed and at room temperature.

How to make Sugar Free Lemon Curd

1.   In a small saucepan on low heat, blend together the lemon juice, zest, and sugar alternative.

2.   When blended, whisk in the eggs and butter. Continuously whisk this as you do not want it to burn and you do not want scrambled eggs with lemon to result. So just remember to whisk while this cooks.

3.   The curd should be thickening while it cooks. When it is thick enough to stick to a spoon (about 5-7 minutes), remove the curd from the heat.

4.   Carefully transfer the curd to a glass (as in nonmetal) bowl. Allow the curd to cool for at least an hour refrigerated.

5.   The curd should keep for about a week when refrigerated.

I am going to try using a sugar free powdered sugar for my sugar alternative in this recipe to get even sweeter taste to balance the tart lemons.

Sugar Free Mascarpone

Mascarpone is the heavenly filing that we enjoy in those wonderful Italian desserts. It is nice to know that it is possible to make a sugar free mascarpone.

Sugar Free Mascarpone

What you need to make Sugar Free Mascarpone

- Heavy Cream- 2 cups.
- Lemon Juice- 1 tablespoon.
- Sugar Alternative- Equivalent to 1 teaspoon of sugar.

How to make Sugar Free Mascarpone

1.   In a small saucepan, simmer the heavy cream at around 180 degrees. Be sure to stir the cream and do not allow it to bubble or burn.

2.   Stir in the lemon juice and allow the saucepan to continue simmering for another 3 1/2 minutes. Stir the mixture as it simmers scraping the sides and bottom as needed to prevent lumping and burning.

3.   Remove the saucepan from the heat. Stir in the sugar alternative. Then cool for 20 minutes. in the saucepan.

4.   For this step, you will need a strainer that is lined with cheesecloth. A sturdy paper towel or coffee filter can work as well. Set the lined strainer in a large measuring cup or similar bowl or cup. Pour the mascarpone from the saucepan into the lined strainer. Lightly cover this and set in the refrigerator overnight.

5. Mascarpone made from home should last a few days when refrigerated.

You could use milk or yogurt or other similar dairy products for the heavy cream. Half and Half is a closer to sugar free alternative choice. Just note that the dairy that you use will affect the consistency of your mascarpone.

Sugar Free Marshmallows

This Sugar Free Marshmallow recipe is one of the most popular recipes on my site. I think the popularity of this recipe may have something to do with the S'Mores, S'Mores dip, and the Sugar Free Rice 'you-know-what' treats recipes on my site.

Sugar Free Marshmallows

What you need to make Sugar Free Marshmallows

- Sugar Free Powdered Sugar- enough for dusting.
- Gelatin Packets- 2 unflavored and unsweetened. This is about 4 tablespoons total.
- Water- 1/2 cup cold.
- Sugar Alternative- equivalent to 2 cups of sugar. I use granular.
- Water- 1/2 cup additional.
- Vanilla Extract- 3 teaspoons.
- Optional Salt- 1/2 teaspoon.

How to make Sugar Free Marshmallows.

1. Prepare a nonmetal baking dish with sugar free powdered sugar by dusting the sugar over the dish. For example, a 9" baking dish. Set the dish aside.

2. In a mixing bowl, combine together the gelatin and the 1/2 cup of cold water. Set this bowl aside, allowing the gelatin and water to thicken and soften together as you work.

3. Next, in a saucepan on medium heat, combine together the sugar alternative, optional salt, and the remaining 1/2 cup of water. Stirring as you go, allow

this to just about bubble (8-10 minutes). Remove the saucepan from the heat and stir in the vanilla.

4.   Now, we will fit the mixer with a whisk and place the the gelatin and cold water mixing bowl in place. Start the mixer on slow or low.

5.   Pour the contents from the saucepan into the mixing bowl. Do this gradually. Allow the mixture to double in size. This can take up to 14 minutes mixing on low so be patient.

6.   One the mixture has doubled in size, you can pour in over the prepped dish from the first step. Evenly distribute the mixture and then sprinkle with additional powdered sugar.

7.   Allow this to cool uncovered. When set and cooled, you can cut your marshmallows into squares. Cool for at least 3 hours, overnight is preferred.

These marshmallows can be easily flavored by swapping out the vanilla extract for another extract. You could also add a bit of food coloring to make them colorful too!

Conclusion

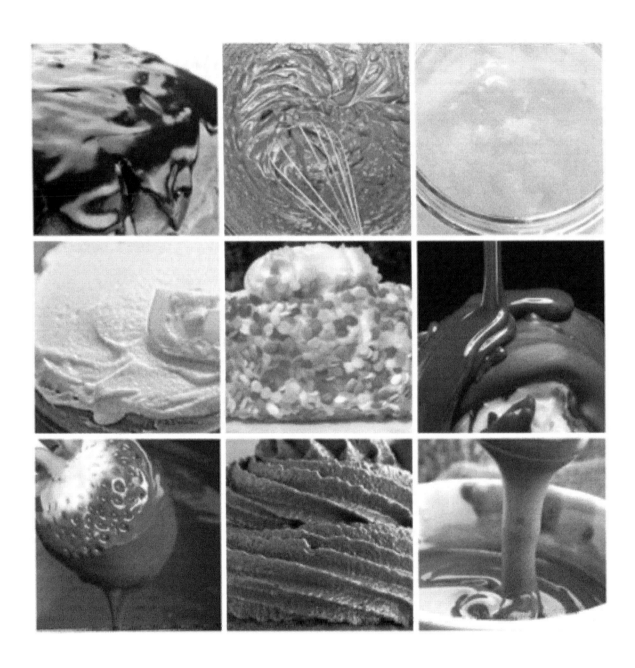

You can certainly enjoy wonderful desserts and treats without all of that added sugar. Learning how to do so may take some trial and error since we are working with sugar alternatives.

For help on how to choose and use sugar alternatives, please check out my Sugar Free Baking Guide that is available on Amazon. The book goes into further depth on the most popular sugar alternatives available. You will learn that not all sugar alternatives are the same.

Even more helpful is the information on which sugar alternatives are best for cooking or baking. Because sugar alternatives do not behave the same as sugar due to their chemical makeup, learning how to use the sugar alternatives can be imperative. The Sugar Free Baking Guide also explains how to measure the sugar alternatives as they are not all 1:1 in equivalency in a recipe to sugar.

Certainly, not all sugar alternatives are calorie free. Some folks prefer a natural sugar alternative as opposed to an artificially manufactured one. Some of these natural choices, such as honey or molasses, do have calories and sugar from their own sources.

You may be wondering why I list sugar alternative amount in a 1:1 equivalence to sugar. This is because many sugar alternatives are sweeter than sugar and thus, you would need less of the sugar alternative than you would need of sugar to achieve a similar sweetness. Because the sugar and the sugar alternatives are parts of the whole volume of a recipe, using less of an alternative than you would use of sugar.

This also brings me to idea of why I prefer granular alternatives to the liquid ones in recipes. In many of my recipes, I find that the granular alternatives produce an end result that is more like the real sugared result because of the dry ingredient volume. Of course there are a few adjustments that may have to be made.

By the way, just because something is sugar free does not mean that it is low in calories. I try to give alternatives to keep my recipes low in carbohydrates or gluten. However, there are recipes (not necessarily mine) that may have higher calorie or fat ingredients added to them to make them seem tasty as they do not have all of the sugar. This is one big reason why I started baking using sugar alternatives.

There are a few recipes that I have made that really do work best with sugar in them. A big example would be a bread recipe that calls for yeast. Yeast needs a bit of sugar to 'ferment' and thus, make a good texture in bread.

In the scheme of servings and that tablespoon or so of sugar that is added to the yeast, you really are not getting a lot of sugar in your slice of bread.

This book is about frostings, icings, and toppings that are made without sugar. If you need more information about any of the recipes you can go to the sugarfreediva.com and find the recipe (use the search box for easiest results). While you are there, you can also find some great recipes, such as cupcakes and cakes, to use with your frosting, icing or topping. Be sure to leave me a comment while you are visiting!

Printed in Great Britain
by Amazon